THE GOLDEN YEARS OF RAILR(

NEW YORK CENTRAL
IN THE HUDSON VALLEY

The Water Level Route in steam and diesel

GEORGE H. DRURY

Distributed by:
Airlife Publishing Ltd.
101 Longden Road, Shrewsbury SY3 9EB, England

Printed in the United States of America

Book Design: Sabine Beaupré
Cover Design: Kristi Ludwig
Copy Editor: Mary Algozin

On the cover: This is the image of the New York Central in the Golden Years: a 4-6-4 pulling a long train of olive green heavyweight coaches and Pullmans along the rock-ballasted four-track Hudson Division. In particular, this is J-1C Hudson No. 5265 with train 22, the eastbound *Lake Shore Limited*, approaching Camelot, New York. Photo by John P. Ahrens, April 16, 1939.

Publisher's Cataloging in Publication
(Prepared by Quality Books, Inc.)
Drury, George H.
New York Central in the Hudson Valley : the Water Level Route in steam and diesel / George H. Drury. — Waukesha, WI : Kalmbach Pub., 1995.
p.   cm.   — (Golden years of railroading ; 2)
Includes bibliographical references and index.
ISBN 0-89024-230-5

1. Railroads—New York (State)—History—Pictorial works. 2. Hudson River Valley (N.Y. and N.J.)—Pictorial works. 3. New York Central Railroad Company—History. I. Title.

TF20.D787 1995   625.1'009'747
                                    QBI95-20346

CONTENTS

Brief history of the New York Central System 5

Grand Central Terminal 11

Hudson Division 27

Harlem Division 85

Putnam Division 97

West Shore 103

West Side Freight Line 113

The lines today 125

Index 127

This is the image of the New York Central in the Golden Years: a 4-6-4 pulling a long train of olive green heavyweight coaches and Pullmans along the rock-ballasted four-track Hudson Division. In particular, this is J-1c Hudson No. 5265 with train 22, the eastbound *Lake Shore Limited*, approaching Camelot, New York. Photo by John P. Ahrens, April 16, 1939.

New York Central

Two companies dominated railroading east of the Mississippi and north of the Ohio and Potomac rivers: the New York Central and the Pennsylvania. New York Central had the edge in route mileage and extent. The New York Central System covered 11,172 route miles at the end of 1929 (660 more than the Pennsy). It reached east as far as Boston and as far north as Montreal, Ottawa, and Mackinaw City, Michigan. Its western limits were St. Louis and Peoria. It reached the Ohio River at Cairo, Illinois (and the Mississippi in the bargain), Evansville, Indiana, and Cincinnati, Ohio; and it had a long tentacle that reached deep into the West Virginia coalfields.

The New York Central System had several subsidiaries. In broad geographic terms, the New York Central Railroad was everything east of Buffalo plus a line from Buffalo through Cleveland and Toledo to Chicago (the former Lake Shore & Michigan Southern). NYC included two leased lines, the Ohio Central Lines (Toledo through Columbus to and beyond Charleston, West Virginia) and the Boston & Albany. West of Buffalo and Cleveland the New York Central System was mostly the province of two almost completely owned subsidiaries, the Michigan Central Railroad and the Big Four (Cleveland, Cincinnati, Chicago & St. Louis Railway). The Michigan Central was a Buffalo-Detroit-Chicago line and everything in Michigan north of that line. The Big Four was everything south of NYC's Cleveland-Toledo-Chicago line that wasn't Ohio Central. New York Central controlled several railroads that were considered part of the New York Central System but were independent to some degree: the Pittsburgh & Lake Erie (Pittsburgh to Youngstown), the Toronto, Hamilton & Buffalo (Welland-Hamilton-Waterford, Ontario), and the Indiana Harbor Belt (from the industrial area at the south end of Lake Michigan west and north to Franklin Park, Illinois). The history of the system is easiest to understand piece by piece.

New York Central

The original New York Central was an upstate company. New York City initially was not infected as severely with railroad fever as Philadelphia and Baltimore were. The rivers that surrounded New York City were its avenues of commerce, and the opening of the Erie Canal in 1825 underscored the importance of shipping. New York City was right on the ocean — Philadelphia and Baltimore were both a considerable distance up long estuaries from the coast — and the Hudson River was navigable for 150 miles inland. New York City didn't need railroads.

In 1825 the Mohawk & Hudson Rail Road was incorporated to join Schenectady with Albany and shortcut the Erie Canal's slow, circuitous route between those cities. The line opened in 1831. Within a few months there was a proposal for a railroad all the way to Buffalo, but the subject was touchy — the state of New York was deeply in debt for the construction of the canal.

The Utica & Schenectady Railroad opened in 1836, and by 1841 a string of railroads stretched from Albany to Buffalo more or less parallel to the Erie Canal. The railroads cooperated early in the matter of through service, and in 1853 12 railroads stretching from Troy and Albany west to Buffalo (ten of them in operation plus two charters for unbuilt railroads) were consolidated to form the New York Central Railroad.

Meanwhile New York City acquired two railroads. The New York & Harlem Railroad was chartered in 1831 to build north from 23rd Street to the Harlem River. Its charter was soon amended to allow it to continue north to Albany. It reached White Plains in 1844 and in 1852 a connection with the Western Railroad at Chatham. The Hudson River Railroad was organized in 1847 by Poughkeepsie interests and was opened in 1851 from the west side of Manhattan to East Albany.

By 1863 Cornelius Vanderbilt controlled the New York & Harlem and had acquired a substantial interest in the Hudson River Railroad. In 1867 he obtained control of the New York Central and in 1869 consolidated it with the Hudson River Railroad to form the New York Central & Hudson River Railroad.

Two groups of lines served the area north of the Albany-Buffalo line. NYC interests built the St. Lawrence & Adirondack Railway north from Herkimer through the Adirondacks to Montreal; a long branch from that line reached northwest to Ottawa. The area along the shore of Lake Ontario was served by a network of branches, the former Rome, Watertown & Ogdensburg Railroad, leased by NYC in 1893 and merged in 1913.

Lake Shore & Michigan Southern

The Michigan Southern Railroad was chartered in 1837 to build across the southern tier of Michigan from a point west of Monroe to New Buffalo on the shore of Lake Michigan. It was built as far west as Hillsdale under state auspices, then was sold to private interests. It was combined with the Erie & Kalamazoo Railroad, which had been opened in 1837 from Toledo, Ohio, northwest to Adrian, Michigan. The new owners extended the Michigan Southern west to meet the Northern Indiana Railroad, which was building eastward from La Porte, Indiana. The line was opened from Monroe through Elkhart, Indiana, to South Bend in 1851, and in early 1852 the line reached Chicago. In 1855 the two roads were combined as the Michigan Southern & Northern Indiana Railroad. By then the company had also completed a direct line between Toledo and Elkhart.

By 1853 NYC controlled the Buffalo & State Line and the Erie & North East railroads, effectively extending NYC to Erie, Pennsylvania. The Cleveland, Painesville & Ashtabula Railroad was opened between Cleveland and Erie in 1852. In 1868 it took its nickname, Lake Shore, as its official name, and in 1869 it absorbed the Cleveland & Toledo Railroad and joined with the Michigan Southern & Northern Indiana to form the Lake Shore & Michigan Southern Railway. Soon afterward Cornelius Vanderbilt acquired control of the LS&MS — and had himself a railroad all the way from New York to Chicago. In 1914 the New York Central & Hudson River, the Lake Shore

& Michigan Southern, and several smaller railroads were combined to form the New York Central Railroad, the second railroad company of that name.

West Shore

In 1880 the New York, West Shore & Buffalo Railroad was organized to build from Jersey City through Albany to Buffalo — parallel to the Central and indeed within sight of it much of the way. William Vanderbilt (who had become president of the NYC&HR upon the death of his father, Cornelius, in 1877) suspected the Pennsylvania Railroad was behind the project — and it was. Construction began, and the line opened in 1883. It was well built and almost gradeless. A rate war ensued and West Shore cut its fares, hoping that NYC would have to do the same and lose great sums of money. But the Central had resources to withstand the temporary loss and West Shore didn't — and entered bankruptcy.

In retaliation, William Vanderbilt revived an old survey for a railroad across southern Pennsylvania that was considerably shorter than the Pennsylvania Railroad's route. Construction began, an expensive project that included nine tunnels.

J. P. Morgan eventually worked a compromise: the Pennsy would get the South Pennsylvania and its tunnels, and NYC would lease the West Shore. NYC got the better deal — the West Shore route along the Hudson proved to be a valuable freight route to the New York City area (most of its Albany-Buffalo line has been abandoned). NYC merged the West Shore Railroad in 1952.

Boston & Albany

The Boston & Worcester Railroad began service between Boston and Worcester, 44 miles, in 1835. In 1840 the Western Railroad opened from Worcester to Springfield and in 1841 to Greenbush, New York, on the east bank of the Hudson opposite Albany. The two roads were consolidated as the Boston & Albany Railroad in 1867. New York Central leased the B&A in 1900 and merged it in 1961. B&A retained more independence than most NYC subsidiaries, and until 1951 its cars and locomotives were lettered Boston & Albany instead of New York Central to placate New England sensibilities.

Ohio Central Lines

The Atlantic & Lake Erie Railroad was chartered in 1869. After a series of financial difficulties and a name change to Ohio Central it managed to link Columbus with the Ohio River at Middleport, Ohio, in 1882. It extended its rails into the coalfields along the Kanawha River in West Virginia and northwest from Columbus to Toledo. It was renamed the Toledo & Ohio Central Railway in 1885. NYC acquired the T&OC in 1910, leased it in 1922, and merged it in 1952. In addition to the T&OC, Ohio Central Lines included three leased roads (all merged in 1938): the Zanesville & Western, the Kanawha & Michigan, and the Kanawha & West Virginia.

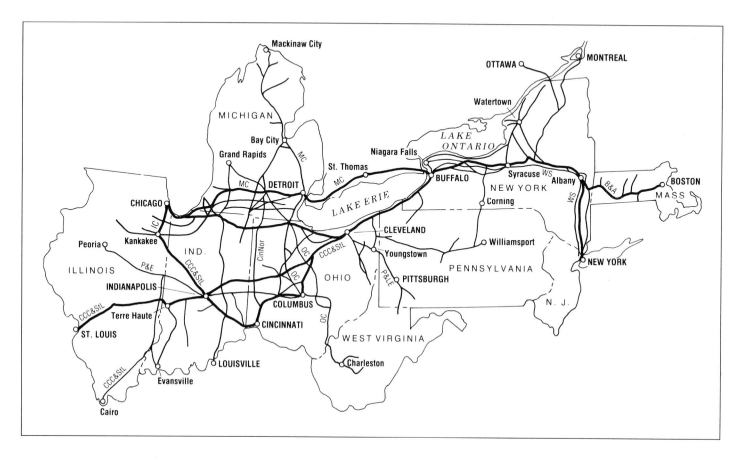

Michigan Central

The Detroit & St. Joseph Railroad was incorporated in 1832 to build a railroad from Detroit to Lake Michigan at St. Joseph. Michigan attained statehood in 1837 and chartered three cross-state railroads: the Southern, from Monroe to New Buffalo, mentioned above; the Northern, from Port Huron to the head of navigation on the Grand River; and the Central, from Detroit to St. Joseph. The state purchased the Detroit & St. Joseph to use as the basis for the Central Railroad.

The railroad ran out of money about the time construction reached Kalamazoo, about three-quarters of the way across the state. Boston interests purchased the railroad from the state and reorganized it as the Michigan Central Railroad. Construction resumed in the direction of New Buffalo instead of St. Joseph, and in 1849 it reached Michigan City, Indiana, about as far as its Michigan charter could take it. The Michigan Central used the charter of a predecessor of the Monon to build a line from Michigan City to the Illinois state line, and it entered Chicago on Illinois Central rails. The line was completed in 1852. Vanderbilt began buying Michigan Central stock in 1869. The Michigan Central also reached east from Detroit across southern Ontario to Buffalo. Vanderbilt first tried to buy the Great Western Railway, a broad-gauge line opened in 1854 from Niagara Falls to Windsor, Ontario. He was unsuccessful and turned his attention to the Canada Southern Railway. He acquired it in 1876, and the Michigan Central leased it in 1882.

Big Four (Cleveland, Cincinnati, Chicago & St. Louis)

The Cleveland, Columbus & Cincinnati Railroad was chartered in 1836. Construction began in 1847, and the line was opened in 1851 from Cleveland to Columbus. In 1852 it teamed up with the Little Miami and Columbus & Xenia to form a Cleveland-Cincinnati route.

In 1848 two railroads, the Indianapolis & Bellefontaine and the Bellefontaine & Indiana, were incorporated to build from Galion, Ohio, on the CC&C, to Indianapolis. The two roads were amalgamated as "The B. Line." They were absorbed in 1868 by the Cleveland, Columbus & Cincinnati when it reorganized as the Cleveland, Columbus, Cincinnati, and Indianapolis Railway (nicknamed "The Bee Line"). By 1872, when it extended its own rails to Cincinnati, the Vanderbilts owned a good chunk of the road's stock. In 1882 the CCC&I acquired control of a line from Indianapolis southwest to St. Louis, and in 1889 it was combined with the Cincinnati, Indianapolis, St. Louis & Chicago Railway (a line from Cincinnati to Kankakee, Illinois, sometimes considered the first "Big Four") to form the Cleveland, Cincinnati, Chicago & St. Louis Railway. The Big Four included a line from Danville, Illinois, south to Cairo, the Peoria & Eastern Railway (Peoria-Indianapolis), and the Cincinnati Northern Railroad (Franklin, Ohio-Jackson, Michigan).

New York Central System

The New York Central leased the Michigan Central and the Big Four in 1930; they remained separate companies to avoid the complexities of merger. In the late 1940s the Chesapeake & Ohio bought a large block of NYC stock and proposed merger. When merger came to the NYC, though, it was not with the C&O but with the Pennsylvania Railroad, NYC's longtime rival. The result of the merger was Penn Central, which began operation on February 1, 1968. On June 21, 1970, PC became the country's largest bankruptcy. That led to the formation of Conrail, which took over the operations of seven railroads on April 1, 1976 — and became profitable in 1981.

Recommended reading:

Road of the Century, by Alvin F. Harlow, published in 1947 by Creative Age Press, New York, New York.

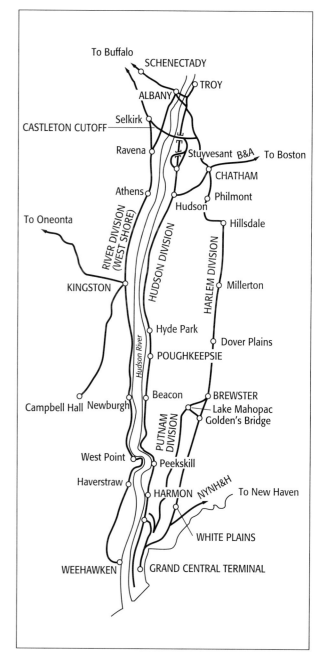

Grand Central Terminal fronts on 42nd Street. Park Avenue divides and its traffic flows past the station on an elevated roadway. NYC photo.

GRAND CENTRAL TERMINAL

Cornelius Vanderbilt wanted a magnificent terminal in New York for his railroads. Because the city of New York had enacted a ruling in 1854 that steam locomotives could not operate south of 42nd Street, Vanderbilt chose a site at Fourth Avenue and 42nd Street, even though that was considered impossibly far uptown.

Construction began in 1869, and Grand Central Depot opened October 8, 1871. Its frontage on 42nd Street was 249 feet, and it stretched almost 700 feet north along Park Avenue. Its facilities included an arched trainshed 200 feet wide and 600 feet long. Somehow Grand Central wound up being three separate stations — if you arrived on the New Haven to leave on a train for Chicago, you had to go outdoors to change trains. That was a minor inconvenience compared to the operational problem of keeping steam locomotives out of the trainshed. Engines cut off inbound trains at speed and the cars were braked to a halt by the crews.

North of Grand Central, Park Avenue was more a busy railroad than a city street. Grade crossings every block created almost infinite possibilities for accidents. A bill was placed before the state legislature asking the railroad to depress its tracks along Park Avenue. The railroad and the city reached a compromise: the city would pay half the cost of depressing the tracks between 49th Street and 96th Street. The tracks were placed in a cut, and two tracks were added to the existing double track. The cut was roofed over, creating a tunnel, and Park Avenue became a boulevard. The project was completed in 1876.

Business increased rapidly, requiring an additional trainshed, the "Annex," opened in 1886, and a complete makeover and enlargement of the building in 1898 (the result of the 1898 project is often referred to as Grand Central Station). That too soon proved inadequate, in large part because of the increase in commuter traffic. Expansion of the existing station was impossible because of the cost of land in Manhattan.

The increase in traffic brought with it another problem: smoke that was not only a nuisance to those living near the tracks but an operational hazard in the Park Avenue tunnel. Engineers often could not see signals (or anything else), and there were several serious accidents. The immediate result of the accidents was that in 1903 the state legislature forbade the use of steam locomotives in Manhattan south of the Harlem River after July 1, 1908.

New York Central had to electrify — there was no other form of motive power that would be practical for the level of traffic. NYC had been studying electrification since 1899 under the leadership of its vice president and chief engineer, William J. Wilgus. There was little practical experience to draw on. The sole heavy-duty mainline railroad electrification was Baltimore & Ohio's 4-mile tunnel at Baltimore, placed in service in 1895, and rapid transit systems in Chicago and New York had begun to electrify.

New York Central adopted the 660-volt third-rail direct-current system used by the B&O and the New York and Chicago elevateds. Tunnel clearances precluded the high-voltage alternating-current system, which had not yet been used for a significant railroad electrification. There was one difference in the NYC electrification. The contact surface of the third rail was underneath, where it would remain free of snow and ice. The top and sides of the third rail could be fully covered with wood for safety.

The electrification project began well before the new station opened. The first electric train operated out of Grand Central on September 30, 1906. Local train service to High Bridge began in December 1906 and to Wakefield on the Harlem Division in January 1907. All trains in and out of Grand Central were electrified by July 1907.

Electrification made possible a new approach to enlarging Grand Central. Land was too expensive to permit widening the station; without the need for open air to disperse smoke from steam engines, the terminal could be double-decked. Wilgus planned a terminal with 31 tracks for long-distance trains on the upper level and 17 tracks for suburban trains on the lower level — plus tracks for loading baggage and mail, storage tracks, and turning tracks that looped around on both levels between the south end of the platforms and 42nd Street. Both levels were below street level so that crosstown streets north of the terminal could be extended across the tracks on bridges. The space over the yards, which covered most of the area from Lexington Avenue to Madison Avenue north as far as 50th Street, would be used for buildings.

Construction was complicated by the fact that the new terminal would be on the site of the one it would replace and train service had to be maintained all the while. Work proceeded from east to west. A new yard was placed in service at the east edge of the site. Several tracks were removed and the area they had occupied was excavated to a depth of 35 to 40 feet. Then the double-deck structure was erected for the new tracks.

The terminal was designed by Reed & Stem of St. Paul, Minnesota, but the project was taken over (with some controversy) by the New York firm of Warren & Wetmore. The new Grand Central Terminal was opened to the public on February 2, 1913.

There were several noteworthy features in the building. Ramps were used instead of stairs to connect the levels, and traffic flow was considered in designing the passageways. The passageways were lined with retail shops of all descriptions (they were a convenience to long-distance and local passengers alike and a source of revenue for the railroad), and the passages extended to nearby office buildings, hotels, and subways.

Gates in the concourse led to departure platforms, but most arriving long-distance trains used a five-track arrival station that was across Vanderbilt Avenue from the main station building. Arriving passengers didn't have to struggle to cross streams of commuters hastening to departing trains.

One Grand Central tradition bears mentioning: the red carpet. For the daily departure of the *20th Century Limited*, NYC's top train, a 260-foot-long carpet was unrolled down the platform from the concourse.

Recommended reading:

Grand Central, by David Marshall, published in 1946 by Whittlesey House (a division of McGraw-Hill), New York, New York.

Grand Central, by William D. Middleton, published in 1977 by Golden West Books, P. O. Box 8136, San Marino, CA 91108. ISBN 0-87095-071-1.

When the Steam Railroads Electrified, by William D. Middleton, published in 1974 by Kalmbach Publishing Co., P. O. Box 1612, Waukesha, WI 53187. ISBN 0-89024-028-0.

The focal point of Grand Central Terminal is the concourse, an enormous room through which flows most of the terminal's traffic. Ticket windows line the south wall of the room. In the center of the concourse is the information booth with the famous gold clock above it. For years New Yorkers said "I'll meet you under the clock."

The second hour hand for daylight saving time in the photo at the right represents the railroads' first concession to the idea of daylight saving time — timetables were still in standard time, but the extra hand on the clock helped passengers translate. The styles worn by the women date the photos as surely as the wartime poster urging "Avoid unnecessary travel" and the advertisement for Frazer automobiles. NYC photos.

Grand Central's lower level served suburban trains. Here passengers wait to board the 5:06 Mount Vernon local on track 102. On track 102A is the 5:05 to Crestwood, which makes its first stop at Mount Vernon (the South Norwalk and Bridgeport destinations at the top of the train indicator are at odds with reality). Photo by David Plowden, March 1960.

The engineer of the *Empire State Express* watches for the conductor's signal to start the train toward Buffalo, Detroit, and Cleveland. The locomotive is a former Cleveland Union Terminal engine that was fitted with third-rail shoes, rewired for 660-volt operation, and moved to New York when CUT's 3000-volt electrification was shut down in 1953. Photo by Jim Shaughnessy, April 13, 1957.

Class P-2B motor No. 223, a former Cleveland Union Terminal locomotive, leads train 1, the *Pacemaker*, into the sunlight at the north portal of the Park Avenue Tunnel (the only portal). The portal was originally at 96th Street; the tunnel was later extended one block north to 97th Street. Photo by Herbert H. Harwood, Jr.

A train of multiple-unit electric cars emerges from the tunnel. NYC photo, about 1953.

Tower NK straddles the four-track elevated line along Park Avenue at 106th Street. Photo by Jim Shaughnessy.

A nine-car train of new multiple-unit cars inbound from the Hudson Division is about to pass under Tower NK. Photo by E. B. Dawson, Jr., November 9, 1951.

Two inbound trains, one locomotive-hauled and the other made up of multiple-unit cars, curve off the Harlem River Bridge and head for 125th Street station, visible a few blocks ahead of the trains. Photo by David Plowden, November 1961.

On the right the *20th Century Limited*, the pride of the New York Central, rolls toward Grand Central, its run from Chicago nearly done. On the left an ancient Class S locomotive hauls the consist of train 6, the *Fifth Avenue* and *Cleveland Limited*, to the coach yard at Mott Haven. Photo by David Plowden, December 1961.

Train 41, the *Knickerbocker*, is barely 5 miles into its trip to St. Louis as it rolls through Mott Haven behind a former Cleveland Union Terminal locomotive. At the left is S-class No. 117, one of NYC's original electric locomotives of 1904. Photo by Herbert H. Harwood, Jr.

ELECTRIC LOCOMOTIVES

NYC had three types of electric locomotives for passenger service. The original locomotives of the Grand Central electrification were the "S motors" — as they were known later. They were built by Alco-GE in three groups in 1904, 1906, and 1908. They were delivered with a 1-D-1 wheel arrangement. Three days after the electric locomotives entered regular service in February 1907 a train derailed and overturned on a curve, killing 23 passengers. The single-axle trucks were suspected, and the locomotives were fitted with two-axle trucks, giving them a 2-D-2 wheel arrangement. They were renumbered as many as four times and reclassed from T to S. Many of them outlived the New York Central.

The S motors weighed 95 tons and were 37 feet long over buffers — not much longer than a General Electric 44-ton diesel switcher (the S-3s were slightly longer and heavier because they had train-heating boilers). Their four bipolar gearless motors gave them a continuous rating of 2200 hp and a starting tractive effort of 32,000 pounds.

Years built	Class as built	Reclassed 1910	Nos. 1904	1905	1908	1917	1936
1904	T-1	S-1	6000	3400	3200	1100	100
1906	T-2	S-2		3401-3434	3201-3234	1101-1134	101-134
1908-1909	T-3	S-3			3235-3246	1135-1146	135-146

Train weights and train speeds soon required more powerful locomotives. Between 1913 and 1926 Alco-GE built 36 T-class locomotives for NYC (the second use of that letter). They had eight axles arranged in a B-B+B-B wheel arrangement. Each was driven by a bipolar, gearless motor of the same type used on the S motors. Starting tractive effort was 69,000 pounds.

Still classed T-2, No. 3424 shows off its new two-axle guiding trucks outside Alco's Schenectady plant. Photo from the collection of C. W. Witbeck.

Engine 222, shown at Harmon, was the first of the Cleveland Union Terminal locomotives to be converted for New York service. Photo by Alfred J. W. McFaddin, March 1955.

Years built	Class	Nos. as built	Renumbered 1936
1913	T-1a	1147	247
1913	T-1b	1148-1156	248-256
1914	T-2a	1157-1162	257-262
1917	T-2b	1163-1172	263-272
1926	T-3a	1173-1182	273-282

The third group of electrics were hand-me-downs from Cleveland Union Terminal. The terminal, opened in 1930, was electrified to eliminate the nuisance of locomotive smoke in downtown Cleveland. NYC passenger trains were pulled by electric locomotives between Collinwood on the east and Linndale on the west, 17 miles (Nickel Plate trains had 5 miles of electric operation from East 40th Street to West 38th Street). CUT had 22 electric locomotives built by Alco and GE in 1929 and 1930. They operated from 3000-volt DC catenary, and they had a 2-C+C-2 wheel arrangement — indeed, they were the first of that wheel arrangement. They were rated at 2635 hp and had a starting tractive effort of 90,000 pounds.

When dieselization of passenger trains rendered CUT's electrics unnecessary, NYC (which owned 93 percent of CUT's stock) rewired the locomotives for low-voltage DC, fitted them with third-rail shoes, and put them in service on the lines into Grand Central.

Years built	Class as built	Reclassed 1955	Nos. as built	Renumbered 1936	1955
1929-1930	P-1a	P-2a	1050-1071	200-221	222-242

No. 220 was destroyed by fire in 1952. No. 218 was rebuilt at Harmon in 1951 and renumbered 222. The other 20 were rebuilt by General Electric at Erie, Pennsylvania, and renumbered in random order.

T-3a No. 1174 is shown on General Electric's test track. The tiny pantographs on the roof are for contacting overhead fourth rail at locations where complicated trackwork require long gaps in the third rail. The round objects on the end platforms are sandboxes. GE photo.

Train 22, the Chicago-New York *Lake Shore Limited*, straightens out briefly on the tangent east of Spuyten Duyvil. Photo by Herbert H. Harwood, Jr.

HUDSON DIVISION

The Hudson River was an admirable artery of commerce — most of the year. During the winter the river froze and the steamboats stopped. The town of Poughkeepsie, about halfway between New York and Albany, observed with some envy that the New York & Harlem Railroad was progressing northward a dozen miles or so east of the Hudson River. More than that, since 1841 the Western Railroad and the Boston & Worcester had constituted an all-weather connection east to Boston for the railroads that reached Albany from the west. The businessmen of Poughkeepsie commissioned surveys south and north, and in 1847 they organized the Hudson River Railroad. They did so over the protests of the steamboat operators, the proprietors of the New York & Harlem, and those who said the railroad would destroy the beauty of the Hudson River (the railroad's argument against the last was that the railroad would smooth off the rough points sticking out into the river and regularize the shoreline where bays indented it and bring a nice symmetry to it all).

The New York & Harlem was well established down the center of Manhattan Island, so the Hudson River Railroad decided to build its line along the west side of the island. Its intention was to run its line as far south as Chambers Street, using horses for motive power below 32nd Street. Construction began at the south end of the line, and at the end of 1849 rails connected New York with Poughkeepsie. The line, laid out by John B. Jervis, was practically gradeless and without sharp curves, and much of it was built double-tracked.

Construction continued northward. The entire line from Albany to Greenbush (which was later named Rensselaer) opened on October 1, 1851. Even before its rails reached Greenbush, the company leased the Troy & Greenbush Railroad, gaining an extension to Troy and a bridge across the Hudson there.

Track and right of way

The mean elevation of the surface of the Hudson at Albany, 150 miles inland, was 6 feet above sea level. New York Central's line along the Hudson was the basis of the road's slogan, "The Water

Level Route." (The Mohawk River and Lake Erie also lay behind that slogan, to which were sometimes appended the words "You can sleep," with the implication that on other railroads you would spend the entire night being hoisted up and down the mountains between Altoona and Pittsburgh.) Much of the route was built with two tracks. By the mid-1940s the line had four tracks from Spuyten Duyvil to just south of Peekskill and from Garrison to Barrytown. From Mott Haven Junction to Spuyten Duyvil it was variously two, three, and four tracks; elsewhere it was double track. At Albany the line widened to four tracks by virtue of the pair of double track bridges across the Hudson, the southerly one leading to the passenger station and the northerly one bypassing it, for freight trains and for passenger trains not making a station stop at Albany.

The line was electrified from Grand Central Terminal to Croton-on-Hudson between 1906 and 1913. (Through trains changed engines at Harmon, 1.18 miles south of Croton-on-Hudson, the end of the Electrified Division and the beginning of the Hudson Division. Employee timetables for 1947 show 4 minutes for the engine change.) Terminals for commuter trains were at Glenwood (a mile north of Yonkers), Croton-on-Hudson, Peekskill, and Poughkeepsie. Glenwood and Croton trains stopped at all stations in the electrified zone; Peekskill and Poughkeepsie trains stopped at only a few stations south of Croton-on-Hudson and at all or nearly all stations north of there.

Branches and connections

The Hudson Division had only one short branch, the connection from Stuyvesant up to the east end of the A. H. Smith Memorial Bridge. At Hudson, 113.7 miles from Grand Central, it connected with a branch of the Boston & Albany from Chatham, and it connected with the New Haven at Beacon, 58.3 miles from Grand Central, Poughkeepsie, 72.8 miles, and Rhinecliff, 88.4 miles. All three New Haven connections were former Central New England lines. The connection at Rhinecliff was gone by the end of the 1930s.

Traffic and operation

The Hudson Division was primarily a passenger railroad. Most of the long-distance trains were scheduled to run overnight, getting their passengers to their destinations at the beginning of the business day. The departures of westbound trains from New York were spread from early afternoon to late evening — a 9 a.m. arrival in St. Louis obviously required a much earlier departure than a train arriving Buffalo at 9 a.m. For eastbound trains the arrival time in New York was the governing factor. Trains from all over the New York Central System converged on the Hudson Division at the same time. An employee timetable for April 1947 shows 15 eastbound trains passing Stuyvesant, 19 miles south of Albany, between 4 and 6:45 a.m. Eastern standard time (in those days the railroads continued to run on standard time even when the rest of the world changed to daylight saving time). That was a train every 11 minutes on the average, with some trains as little as 5 minutes apart. Six of those trains bypassed the Albany station and changed crews in the

Rensselaer yard. Most westbound trains stopped at Albany; during the small hours of the morning a few made the crew-change stop at Rensselaer instead.

Castleton Cutoff

The Albany station, the Rensselaer engine terminal, the two bridges, and junctions with the Boston & Albany, the NYC branch to Troy, and the Delaware & Hudson were concentrated in a small area on the banks of the Hudson. The station was cramped, making switching difficult, and the 8-mile-long stretch of 1.6 percent grade up West Albany Hill started at the north throat of the station. Most passenger and freight trains required pushers. Congestion was almost continuous.

As early as the mid-1870s Cornelius Vanderbilt contemplated the idea of an Albany bypass, using the Athens Branch (formerly the Saratoga & Hudson River Railway), a new high-level crossing of the Hudson south of Athens, and a link to the New York & Harlem. The grades of the New York & Harlem would have been a handicap to heavy traffic, and the city of Albany opposed the idea because it would remove business from the city.

By 1910 the situation at Albany needed relief. The NYC began to look for alternate routes through the Albany area, and in 1913 it formed the Hudson River Connecting Railroad to build the new lines. Since the project included a bridge across a navigable waterway, the approval of the United States Secretary of War was necessary — and obtained in 1917 — but the state of New York withdrew its previous approval of the project. The railroad felt that federal approval superseded state disapproval and made the necessary plans, but construction did not begin until 1922, when Congress passed special legislation.

The most conspicuous part of the project was the A. H. Smith Memorial Bridge across the Hudson south of the town of Castleton-on-Hudson, 9 miles south of Albany. (Smith was president of the New York Central from 1914 to 1924.) With its approaches the bridge was a mile long; the tracks were 150 feet above the river. From the east end of the bridge a connecting line dropped down to the Hudson Division at Stuyvesant, 19 miles south of Albany, with a flying junction to permit southbound trains to enter the main line without delaying or waiting for northbound trains.

Another connecting line went east 7 miles to connect with the Boston & Albany, by then part of the New York Central System, at Niverville. West of the bridge a new line crossed the West Shore's Albany Branch at Selkirk, then led into a new 6-mile-long freight yard — Selkirk Terminal Yard. The west end of Selkirk Yard was connected to the West Shore's main line. From Rotterdam Junction on the West Shore a line crossed the river to NYC's main line at Hoffman's, 26 miles west of Albany. The project was completed in November 1924.

Recommended reading:

Rails Along the Hudson, edited by Thomas M. Crawford and Frederick A. Kramer, published in 1979 by Quadrant Press, 19 West 44th Street, New York, NY 10036. ISBN 0-915276-25-9.

A T-1B locomotive leads a Poughkeepsie local along the Harlem River between Marble Hill and Spuyten Duyvil. Photo by Jim Shaughnessy, April 13, 1957.

A train led by a pair of NYC's first group of MU cars curves through the rock cut between Spuyten Duyvil and Marble Hill. Photo by Herbert H. Harwood, Jr.

Engine 222, the first of the Cleveland motors to be rebuilt, brings train 1, the *Pacemaker*, an overnight New York-Chicago coach train, through the rock cut east of Spuyten Duyvil. Photo by Herbert H. Harwood, Jr.

Venerable MU cars accelerate eastward after the station stop at Spuyten Duyvil. The bridge overhead carries the Henry Hudson Parkway; beyond is the drawbridge of the West Side Freight Line. Photo by Herbert H. Harwood, Jr.

A train of MU cars heading for Grand Central rolls around the curve into the Spuyten Duyvil station. The reverse curves of the roof over the westbound platform are a whimsical addition to the antique board-and-batten station building. Photo by Herman Rinke.

Train 2, the *Pacemaker* from Chicago, rounds the Spuyten Duyvil curve.
At the left of the photo is DV tower, which controls the junction.
Photo by John Pickett, August 1963.

A New York-bound train of MU cars (built by St. Louis Car Co. in 1951) turns away
from the Hudson River into the station at Spuyten Duyvil.
Photo by Jim Shaughnessy, April 13, 1957.

Train 1, the *Pacemaker*, shows off two classes of NYC electric passenger locomotives: Lightning-striped 226 is a former Cleveland Union Terminal engine, and 275 is NYC's own class T, with a B-B+B-B wheel arrangement. Both photos by Herbert H. Harwood, Jr.

It's 9:15 in the morning and train 51, the *Empire State Express*, is half an hour out of Grand Central at Greystone with motor 226 in charge. Photo by John Pickett, August 1963.

A work train moves south on the outside track just north of Spuyten Duyvil behind a K-11 Pacific. Photo by Arthur F. Knauer, April 18, 1947.

An airline strike has swollen the consist of the Chicago-bound *20th Century Limited* to 17 cars. Sleeper-observation car *Hickory Creek* brings up the rear. Photo by John Pickett, August 1966.

The St. Louis-bound *Knickerbocker* rolls north through Tarrytown on the express track behind T-class motor No. 278. Photo by David Plowden, April 1955.

Train 40, the eastbound *Missourian* from St. Louis, is on the express track at Scarborough. T motor 282 is in charge. Photo by David Plowden, May 1955.

A trio of MU cars built by St. Louis in 1951 starts toward New York from the station at Harmon. Photo by Jim Shaughnessy, April 13, 1957.

A Poughkeepsie-New York local arrives at Harmon, where it will trade its Alco RS-3 for an electric locomotive. On the right is a pair of E7s waiting for train 55, the *Advance Empire State Express*. In the distance is an RDC-1 used on Harmon-Peekskill and Harmon-Poughkeepsie shuttles. Photo by David Plowden, March 1955.

A pair of RDC-1s is ready to depart as a late-evening Harmon-Peekskill shuttle train. Photo by Jim Shaughnessy.

Train 134, the *Laurentian*, prepares to depart Harmon on the last leg of its Montreal-New York run, behind P-2B motor 232. Photo by Jim Shaughnessy.

Niagara 6017 starts out of Harmon with train 39, the *North Shore Limited*, for Detroit and Chicago. A single streamlined coach is the fifth car in the otherwise all-heavyweight consist. Photo by Frank Quin, March 1946.

The train and the place are the same, the *North Shore Limited* at Harmon, but several years have passed in this photo of an unlikely motive power combination, a Fairbanks-Morse Erie-built A unit and an Electro-Motive F3 B unit. Photo by Jim Shaughnessy.

Pacific 4742, a K-3, accelerates north from Harmon with a six-coach consist, probably a local train for Peekskill or Poughkeepsie. Photo by Frank Quin, 1940.

4-6-4 — HUDSON

New York Central owned more than half of all the 4-6-4s built for service in North America, and that distinction was appropriate, since NYC was the first to put that wheel arrangement in service.

The standard passenger locomotive of the early 1920s was the Pacific. The success of Lima Locomotive Works' Super-Power 2-8-4 of 1925 implied that a four-wheel trailing truck and the larger firebox and greater steaming capacity it would allow would be as beneficial to a passenger engine as to a freight engine.

Credit for designing the first 4-6-4 is usually given to the Chicago, Milwaukee & St. Paul, which drew up plans for such a locomotive in 1925. However, the Milwaukee Road soon thereafter entered bankruptcy and shelved its plans for new passenger locomotives until 1929.

The New York Central had pushed the 4-6-2 to the limits imposed by its track and clearances, but passenger train weights continued to increase. In November 1926 NYC experimentally applied a four-wheel trailing truck to a K-3 Pacific and at the same time ordered a single 4-6-4 from American Locomotive Company.

Number 5200 emerged from Alco's Schenectady Works on February 14, 1927. The new locomotive carried slightly less weight on its 79-inch drivers than NYC's K-3 Pacific but more on the trailing truck, which supported a much larger firebox. After extensive testing, NYC ordered 59 more Hudsons — and named the type for the river NYC follows from New York to Albany. Within four years the New York Central system had 165 4-6-4s — 145 J-1s like 5200 and 20 75-inch drivered J-2s on subsidiary Boston & Albany. In 1937 the Central received 40 J-3s, which had the same basic specifications. Differences included a conical boiler, a shorter smokebox, a combustion chamber ahead of the firebox, smaller cylinders, and higher boiler pressure; 10 streamlined J-3s came in 1938, making 275 in all.

Hudson 5297 was a J-1d, built by Alco in 1929.
Photo from the collection of F. H. Howard.

The Hudsons' successors

New York Central freight locomotive development moved in two directions in the 20th century. For slow freight trains NYC used first the 2-8-0, then the 2-8-2. For fast freight, chiefly perishable foodstuffs, NYC used the 4-6-2 in 1910; it had been using Pacifics in passenger service since 1903. In 1916 NYC turned to the 4-8-2 for fast freight. By 1930 it had 485 4-8-2s on its roster — and they were Mohawks, not Mountains. In the late 1930s Mohawks were occasionally called on to substitute for Hudsons in passenger service. As built, they were limited to 60 mph. NYC rebuilt two with lightweight rods, disk drivers, and improved counterbalancing and found that they could run as fast as the Hudsons. Between 1940 and 1943 NYC bought 115 more 4-8-2s, 25 intended specifically for passenger work but equally useful in freight service. The Hudsons that were displaced by new Mohawks in turn replaced Pacifics, and some Hudsons were used in freight service in their last years.

NYC was pleased with its dual-service Mohawks but wanted more boiler capacity, which meant a larger firebox supported by a four-wheel trailing truck — a 4-8-4. The 27 Niagaras that Alco delivered in 1945 and 1946 were the ultimate development of the steam passenger locomotive on the New York Central. In a series of tests they were found to be the equal of a three-unit E7 passenger diesel if they were given extra attention and priority treatment by roundhouse crews — but the diesels didn't need extra attention and priority treatment.

Class	Nos. as built	Later Nos.	Builder	Dates built	Built for
J-1a–J-1e	5200-5344	5200-5344	Alco	1927-1931	NYC
J-1b, c, d	8200-8229	5345-5374	Alco	1927-1930	MC
J-1d, e	6600-6629	5375-5404	Alco	1929, 1931	CCC&StL
J-2a, b	600-609	5455-5464	Alco	1928, 1930	B&A
J-2c	610-619	5465-5474	Lima	1931	B&A
J-3a	5405-5454	5405-5454	Alco	1937-1938	NYC

Built streamlined: 5445-5454 (*20th Century Limited*)
Streamlined later: 5344 (named *Commodore Vanderbilt*, later restreamlined to look like the *20th Century Limited* engines), 5426 and 5429 (*Empire State Express*)
Sold to Toronto, Hamilton & Buffalo: 5311 and 5313

J-3a Hudson 5423 rounds a curve along the bank of the Hudson just north of Harmon with the all-coach *Pacemaker* to Chicago. Conversion from semaphores to searchlight signals is under way.
Photo by Frank Quin, 1942.

Another J-3a, No. 5420, leads the *Ohio State Limited*, heading for Columbus and Cincinnati, through Oscawanna. Photo by Theo. A. Gay, June 15, 1946.

Hudson 5451, one of the ten J-3a-class engines that were built streamlined, wheels the *20th Century Limited*, train 25, through Oscawanna. Photo by W. W. Curtis, August 10, 1941.

Even though freight traffic on the Hudson Division was secondary to passenger traffic, the amount of freight traffic would do credit to many a main line elsewhere in the country. Mohawk 3148, built by Lima in 1944, speeds New York-bound perishables through Oscawanna. The two cars just ahead of the caboose are poultry cars, carrying live chickens. Photos by Theo. A. Gay, June 15, 1946.

Niagara 6019, less than a year old, has the 17 cars of train 49, the *Advance Knickerbocker*, moving at good speed. Photo by Theo. A. Gay, June 15, 1946.

Several years later and later in the day, Hudson 5202, the third of its class, pinch-hits for a diesel on train 65, the *Advance Commodore Vanderbilt*. Photo by Frank Quin.

New York Central owned more Alco freight cab units than any other road. Here a matched FA-2/FB-2/FA-2 set leads a freight train north through Oscawanna. Photo by Bert Pennypacker, 1952.

A pair of Electro-Motive F7s has been deputized into extra passenger service with a long train of heavyweight Pullmans. The train is about to enter the tunnel just north of Oscawanna. Photo by David W. Salter, August 1952.

A northbound local train for Albany departs Crugers behind Hudson 5255. Photo by John F. McBride.

Two Hudsons stand side by side for a moment at Peekskill: 5226 on a local train and 5269 on the Utica-New York *Upstate Special*. Photo by Herb Weisberger, 1942.

A streamlined J-3a Hudson is far removed from the *20th Century Limited* duties for which it was built as it leads a southbound local train at Peekskill. Photo by Herb Weisberger, December 1944.

Train 58, the *Niagara* from Chicago and Detroit, rolls south across the drawbridge at Peekskill.
Photo by Wayne Brumbaugh, July 4, 1938.

At Roa Hook just north of Peekskill the New York-bound *Upstate Special* leans into a curve behind Niagara 6017.
Photo by James D. Bennett.

Hudsons 5303 and 5204 lead milk train 185 and the Montreal-bound *Laurentian* northward under the east end of the Bear Mountain Bridge. Both photos by Wayne Brumbaugh.

The Bear Mountain Bridge affords a fine view of the Hudson Valley and of activity on the Water Level Route: a single E8 with a southbound ten-car train, and the *Commodore Vanderbilt* heading for Albany and Chicago. Just ahead of the *Brook*-series observation car is a Union Pacific sleeper to San Francisco. Photo of the *Commodore* by O. Winston Link, July 1957.

The Hudson Division has a number of short tunnels like this one through Anthony's Nose Mountain. The approaching train is southbound. Photo by F. Eidenbenz.

Alco PAs have a section of the *20th Century Limited* rolling south at Garrison. Photo by John F. McBride.

The eastbound *Century* is shown between Cold Spring and Garrison only 18 days after the inaugural run of the streamlined equipment. Photo by Wayne Brumbaugh, July 3, 1938.

When diesels were first assigned to the *Century* they were painted to match the prewar livery of the train, light gray with a dark gray window band. The next-to-last car of the 16-car train is a Santa Fe sleeping car bound for Los Angeles via the *Chief*. Photo by Robert R. Malinoski, August 11, 1946.

Lined up at Harmon waiting for westbound trains are three sets of passenger diesels led by E7 4034, PA-1 4202, and E7 4007, which wears an early version of NYC's lightning-stripe livery in which the light and dark gray are reversed and the nose stripes are closer together and run higher up the nose. NYC photo.

Lesser trains were often a mixture of stainless steel, two-tone gray, and heavyweight cars, but until coaches were added to its consist in 1958, the *20th Century Limited* was recognizable by the uniformity of its appearance, as shown here at Cold Spring: two-tone gray from the nose of the diesel or the bullet nose of the streamlined Hudson to the round end of the observation car. NYC photo, June 13, 1950.

The *Empire State Express*, a daytime train between New York, Cleveland, and Detroit, received streamlined cars and locomotives on December 7, 1941. It is shown on a press run at Breakneck Mountain. The makeup of the train was unconventional in that parlor car passengers rode up front and coach passengers to the rear — with a tavern-observation car for coach passengers. NYC photos.

A class L-2 Mohawk pops out of the tunnel through Breakneck Mountain south of Beacon with a northbound freight. "Mountain" was the usual name for the 4-8-2 type — but that wouldn't do on the Water Level Route. Photo by T. J. Donahue, 1947.

Two Fairbanks-Morse Erie-builts are in charge of the *Knickerbocker* at Breakneck Mountain. The train is a secondary New York-St. Louis train with a mixture of coaches and sleepers, heavyweight and lightweight construction, and gray paint and stainless steel. It will pick up additional cars during the night at Buffalo, Cleveland, and Indianapolis. Photo by C. M. Bovid, March 18, 1951.

Pacific 4569 pauses with its local freight opposite Storm King Mountain. Photo by Raymond C. Henry, 1942.

Two of New York Central's first group of E7s, 4002 and 4003, were delivered in an experimental paint scheme: black with a modest amount of white striping. The two are shown at Camelot on the *Missourian*, a St. Louis-New York secondary train that shed most of its sleeping cars at Cleveland and Buffalo. Photo by John P. Ahrens, August 1947.

Hudson 5222 leads a long milk train northward at Camelot — empties returning for a refill. Two daily milk trains in each direction were scheduled along the Hudson Division and the West Side Freight Line in the late 1940s. Photo by John P. Ahrens, August 1947.

Niagara 6012 has train 41, the *Knickerbocker*, moving at speed at Camelot. The consist of the train includes conventional heavyweight and prewar and postwar lightweight streamlined cars. Photo by John P. Ahrens, July 4, 1947.

An E8 and an E7 lead a southbound train into the Poughkeepsie station. The first 11 cars at least are mail and express; there are four Flexi-Van cars in the consist. In the background is the bridge that carries New Haven's Maybrook line across the Hudson. Photo by Jim Shaughnessy.

E7s 4022 and 4025 are on the point of train 39, the *North Shore Limited*, at Rhinecliff. The train will reach Buffalo mid-evening and Detroit in the small hours of the morning. There it will pick up coaches and sleepers brought from Toronto by Canadian Pacific, then proceed west across Michigan to Chicago. Photo by Joseph R. Quinn, June 25, 1951.

The *Mohawk*, train 142, pauses at Barrytown, 94 miles from Grand Central and the north end of a long section of four-track line. Photo by Raymond C. Henry, 1938.

Track pans were placed at intervals along the line so that trains could take water without stopping. Hudson 5328 demonstrates the art of scooping water at Tivoli. The train is No. 40, the *Mohawk*. Photo by William D. Middleton, September 1949.

A New York-bound freight rolls off the connection from the A. H. Smith Memorial Bridge onto the Hudson Division main line at Stuyvesant behind Mohawk 3115. The connection for northbound trains has an easier grade and begins its climb opposite the north end of the station platform. Photo by R. E. Tobey, September 1948.

The *Laurentian*, the day train from Montreal, speeds south at approximately the same spot.
The signal gantry in the distance marks the point where the southbound freight connection
joins the main line. Photo by R. E. Tobey.

This view of the A. H. Smith Memorial Bridge from the northwest shortly after construction shows how New York Central took advantage of the peninsula between Binnen Kill and the Hudson on the west bank and Lower Schodack Island on the east bank. NYC photo.

Train 39 is about to pass underneath the A. H. Smith Memorial Bridge between Schodack Landing and Castleton. The lead diesel unit is an E8; the second unit is a PB-1 that has been repowered with an Electro-Motive engine. Photo by Jim Shaughnessy.

Hudson 5210 passes SK Tower at the east end of Selkirk Yard with a freight heading down the West Shore.
Photo by William D. Middleton, May 21, 1950.

A freight powered by a Mohawk has just climbed the connecting line from Stuyvesant and is passing SM Tower at the east end of the A. H. Smith Memorial Bridge. The tower marks the dividing line between the Hudson Division, the Mohawk Division, and the Albany Division of the Boston & Albany. NYC photo.

A northbound freight meets a southbound local passenger train on the line between Rensselaer and Troy. Photo by Gene Baxter.

The southbound *Laurentian* from Montreal has just arrived in Troy Union Station on a winter afternoon. New York Central power waits in the distance for the Delaware & Hudson road-switcher to cut off. The stainless-steel NYC parlor observation car looks road-weary, but its drumhead displays the train name. NYC, D&H, and Boston & Maine shared the station. Photo by Jim Shaughnessy.

E8 4089 replenishes its water tank at Albany before heading down the Hudson with train 2, the *Pacemaker*.
Photo by Jim Shaughnessy, March 1959.

Train 95 has just arrived in Albany from New York. The rear cars, including the stainless-steel parlor observation car, will be pulled off to form Delaware & Hudson train 35, the *Laurentian* to Montreal; the remainder of 95 will continue west as a local train to Syracuse. The ornate building in the background is D&H's general office building. Photo by Philip R. Hastings.

Train 2, the *Pacemaker* from Chicago, rolls past Tower B at the north end of Albany station. The leading E8 is notable for carrying a short-lived version of the NYC oval herald that preceded the "cigar-band" herald. Photo by Jim Shaughnessy, March 1959.

The westbound *Empire State Express* prepares to depart Albany for Buffalo, Cleveland, and Detroit. The E7 and the PA-1 face the hardest task of their day, the climb up West Albany Hill.
Photo by Jim Shaughnessy, March 1959

A train of brand-new multiple-unit electric cars curves past the platform at White Plains on a test run before entering revenue service. The top and sides of the third rail, which supplies 660-volt direct current, are covered with wood for safety; the current collector shoes run along the bottom surface of the third rail. New York Central photo, 1950.

HARLEM DIVISION

New York's first railroad was the New York & Harlem Railroad, chartered in 1831 to run the length of Manhattan Island, from 23rd Street north to the Harlem River, with a branch to the Hudson River near 125th Street. The charter specified an alignment somewhere between Third Avenue and Eighth Avenue; the company chose Fourth Avenue. Construction began with a ceremonial blast of black powder to begin the cut through Murray Hill. Even at that ground-breaking ceremony there was mention of building the railroad north to Albany. The city government prescribed numerous conditions and restrictions, one of which was that south of 14th Street trains would be drawn only by horses, and the initial function of the New York & Harlem was to provide horse-car service in the city. Rails reached the Harlem River in 1837.

In 1840 the charter was amended to allow the company to build north through Westchester County to connect with the New York & Albany Railroad (which had been chartered to build north from the end of the NY&H but thus far hadn't built anything) and also to build a branch east to connect with railroads in Connecticut.

The New York & Harlem's track reached White Plains in December 1844. Construction continued northward, spurred in part by the Hudson River Railroad, which began construction in 1846. In January 1852 the NY&H made a junction with the Western Railroad at Chatham, 128 miles from New York. Nearer New York, the railroad soon developed a good commuter business.

In 1842 Gouverneur Morris, a director of the New York & Harlem, built his own 2-mile railroad from the NY&H at Melrose to his property at Port Morris on the East River. The New York & Harlem purchased the line in 1853. Another branch was completed in 1871 from Mott Haven along the Harlem River and Spuyten Duyvil Creek to the Hudson River.

The place where motive power changed from horses to steam moved north through the years. The city enacted an ordinance in 1844 moving the southerly limit of steam operation to 32nd Street, where a roundhouse had been erected. The railroad got an extension of the effective date several times until the city enacted another ordinance in 1851 making it 42nd Street. The railroad leased its right of way south of there to a local company for horsecar and later electric car and bus operation.

The New York & New Haven, building westward, met the New York & New Haven at Mount Vernon in 1848, and its trains began running into New York on Harlem rails.

Corporate

By the mid-1840s Cornelius Vanderbilt had acquired stock in several railroads in the area, and after 1850 he started buying New York & Harlem stock. About that time the company came into financial difficulty through the work of unscrupulous management — out-and-out dishonest management, to be accurate. More than that, city government was corrupt and threatening removal of tracks from streets, prohibition of steam locomotives, and increased

CORNELIUS VANDERBILT (1794-1877) was born into a farming family on Staten Island. He received little education and went to work early. At 16 he bought a small boat and began ferry service between Staten Island and Manhattan. In 1813 he married Sophia Johnson, a cousin, and began to build a family that eventually numbered nine daughters and four sons (one of whom died in infancy). His ferry business prospered and expanded, first to New Brunswick, New Jersey, then out Long Island Sound to Stonington, Connecticut. His shipping interests later included a system of ships and stage-coaches from New York to California via Nicaragua and a transatlantic route. Vanderbilt's shipping activities got him the nickname "Commodore."

He held directorships of several of the railroads that connected with his boats. In 1857 he acquired control of the New York & Harlem Railroad. It was a weak railroad; its chief asset was its line the length of Manhattan Island. In 1863 he bought control of the Hudson River Railroad, and in 1864 he bought a block of New York Central stock. He attempted to gain control of the Erie in 1867 but failed; the event was his only unsuccessful bid to acquire a railroad. Throughout his later years he continued to buy NYC stock to maintain control of the road.

The Commodore was concerned about the future of his railroad empire, and he arranged his will so that nearly all of his $100 million estate went to his son William H. and to William's sons, in particular Cornelius II. The Commodore died in 1877 and was buried in the family vault in a Moravian cemetery on Staten Island.

franchise fees. Vanderbilt was elected to the board of directors. Almost immediately the railroad asked for a loan, with which he obliged — and he became a permanent part of the management.

In 1873 the New York Central & Hudson River Railroad leased the New York & Harlem Railroad and began operating it. The lease passed successively to New York Central, Penn Central, Conrail, and Metro-North — the New York & Harlem Railroad still exists as a corporation, owned almost entirely by Penn Central Company.

Track and right of way

The New York & Harlem was not a spectacular, showy piece of railroad engineering. The line followed a series of small river valleys northward through increasingly hilly country. For about 15 miles between Millerton and Hillsdale the line lay along the foot of the steep west slope of the Taconic Mountains, which rose more than 1,000 feet above the railroad. The line reached its highest point, 776 feet above sea level, a little north of the Mount Riga station. Despite the hilly country, the grades along the lines were not steep. The longest sustained grades were three stretches about 7 miles long and ranging from 0.5 to 0.7 percent: north through Brewster, north through Millerton to Mount Riga, and south from Philmont. The steepest grade on New York & Harlem was 3,300 feet of 1.02 percent — not in the mountains at the corner of New York, Connecticut, and Massachusetts but in the Park Avenue Tunnel at 86th Street.

As part of the Grand Central Terminal project the Harlem Division was electrified. Electric service began between Grand Central and Wakefield, a mile south of Mount Vernon, on January

WILLIAM HENRY VANDERBILT (1821-1885) was the Commodore's oldest son. During his youth he was a disappointment to his father, who considered him dull and backward. Soon after William married Maria Kissam his health failed, and the Commodore installed him on a marginal farm on Staten Island. When William made a success of the farm and was able to enlarge it, his father began to think better of him. William was later made manager of the Staten Island Railroad, one of the Commodore's properties, and soon was brought onto the board of the New York & Harlem. In 1883 William resigned from the presidency of the NYC because of failing health — high blood pressure, a stroke, and blindness in one eye. He owned 87 percent of the stock of the railroad and asked J. P. Morgan if he could sell the majority of it without causing a panic. He did so with the condition that he or his nominee hold a seat on NYC's board. William retained his interest in the South Pennsylvania Railroad. A few days after the South Penn-West Shore affairs was resolved in 1885, William was conversing in his office with Robert Garrett, president of the Baltimore & Ohio, and suddenly collapsed and died.

Other members of the Vanderbilt family who were active in New York Central affairs include William Henry's sons Cornelius II (1843-1899), William Kissam (1849-1920), and Frederick William (1856-1938); William Kissam's sons William Kissam, Jr., (1878-1944) and Harold S. (1884-1970), the last Vanderbilt to serve on NYC's board of directors; the Commodore's sons-in-law Daniel Torrance and Horace F. Clark; and William Henry's son-in-law William Seward Webb.

28, 1907. The electrification reached White Plains in 1910. That was to remain the north end of the third rail through the New York Central and Penn Central administrations.

The Park Avenue tunnel and viaduct carried four tracks, and the four tracks continued north on the Harlem Division to Mount Vernon. Early on, the line was double-tracked to White Plains North; the second track reached Golden's Bridge in 1902 and Brewster in 1909. Until 1948 double track continued north from Brewster to the summit of the grade at Dykeman's, 2 miles north of Brewster.

In electrified territory passenger trains were allowed a maximum speed of 55 mph. North of White Plains the limit was 60, except for lower speeds on the curves that abounded between White Plains and Brewster and a 50-mph limit for the same reason between Martindale and Ghent.

Branches and connections

The Harlem Division had two short branches and only a few connections with railroads that weren't other parts of the New York Central. NYC's main route to Albany — it became the Hudson Division at Croton-on-Harmon — diverged westward at Mott Haven Junction, 5.4 miles from Grand Central. At the junction was the coach yard that serviced the trains that originated and terminated at Grand Central. It was one of the busiest such yards in the nation.

The Port Morris Branch, which diverged to the east at Melrose, 6.1 miles from Grand Central, is still active as a freight line. During the years Franklin Roosevelt was in the White House, it was part of the route Roosevelt traveled between Washington and his home in Hyde Park north of

Poughkeepsie. The Pennsylvania took his train from Washington to Pennsylvania Station, New York, and the New Haven took it from there through the East River tunnels and over Hell Gate Bridge to Port Morris. From there the New York Central took it west to the Harlem Division at Melrose, then south to Mott Haven Junction, and west and north on the Hudson Division.

At Woodlawn, 11.8 miles from Grand Central, the New Haven branched to the east. In 1910 a flyover was built to allow westbound New Haven trains to reach the eastward tracks of the Harlem Division without disturbing traffic on the westward tracks. (NYC trains heading to New York were eastward by the timetable, southward by the compass.)

The next junction north was with the branch to Lake Mahopac at Golden's Bridge, 43.5 miles from Grand Central. The 7.2-mile branch was opened in 1871 by the New York & Mahopac Railroad, which was owned by the New York & Harlem (and leased to it in 1872). The branch crossed the Putnam Division less than a mile before its end at a point named XC. Trains on the branch faced an ascending grade averaging 2 percent most of the way. Until April 1, 1959, a few Harlem Division trains operated via Mahopac, using the branch between Golden's Bridge and XC and the upper end of the Putnam Division between XC and Putnam Junction.

Most commuter trains terminated at Brewster, 51.9 miles from Grand Central. The Putnam Division entered the Harlem Division from the west at a point named Putnam Junction just north of Brewster station. Putnam Division and Harlem Division trains for New York departed Brewster in opposite directions. In 1881 the New York & Northern, a predecessor of the Putnam Division, built a bridge over the Harlem Division to effect a junction with the New York & New England. The bridge was destroyed by fire shortly after the turn of the century, by which time the through service offered by the NY&N and NY&NE was long gone.

About 6 miles north of Brewster at Towners the New York & New England (later the New Haven's line from Devon, Connecticut, to Maybrook, New York) crossed over the Harlem on a through truss bridge.

At Millerton, 92.7 miles from Grand Central, Mount Riga, 95.8, and Boston Corners, 99.7, the Harlem met the Central New England (to use its turn-of-the-century identity). From Millerton lines ran east to Winsted and Hartford and southwest to Beacon. From Boston Corners CNE lines ran west to Rhinecliff, southwest to Poughkeepsie and Maybrook, and southeast parallel to the Harlem to State Line, just east of Millerton. The CNE was the result of several efforts to connect Hartford to the Hudson River, the Erie Railroad, and the Delaware & Hudson Canal and later to transport Pennsylvania anthracite to New England. The New Haven purchased the CNE in 1904 to get its only important component, the bridge over the Hudson at Poughkeepsie. Most of the CNE, including lines that connected with the Harlem Division, was abandoned by 1939.

The Harlem encountered no other railroads until it reached Ghent, 25 miles north of Boston Corners. Between there and Chatham the Harlem paralleled the Boston & Albany's Chatham-Hudson branch. In 1907 the two lines were paired to form double track, an arrangement that lasted until 1937.

The Harlem Division ended at Chatham and connected there with the Boston & Albany's main line and a secondary line of the Rutland to Bennington.

Traffic

The Harlem Division was primarily a passenger railroad: Monday-to-Friday commuters, people going down to New York for the day, and weekend traffic to the Berkshires and the Taconics. The Harlem Division and the Boston & Albany cooperated to run through trains between western Massachusetts and New York City in competition with the New Haven. The New York-Chatham-Pittsfield-North Adams trains were the premier passenger trains on the Harlem and carried parlor and dining cars (a few New York-Chatham trains also carried diners).

The Harlem Division and the B&A also combined to serve as a detour route between New York and Albany when the Hudson Division was blocked — by a derailment, perhaps, or flooding.

In early years cemeteries at Kenisco and Mount Pleasant generated considerable business for the Harlem Division, not only visitors but one-way traffic. Valhalla was the station to which remains were consigned, and even through the 1960s the Official Guide noted that "Remains may be checked to Valhalla, however advance notice must be given to Baggage Agent, Grand Central Terminal."

Freight traffic was primarily local; traffic to and from New York City moved on the Hudson and River divisions. Milk traffic was important. The Harlem Division traversed dairy country, and Borden had numerous plants along the line. The line also received milk trains from the Rutland at Chatham, until a federal marketing order in 1958 restricted Vermont dairies from selling milk to the New York area.

Operations

New York-White Plains trains, which were operated with electric cars, stopped at all or nearly all the stations. New York-Brewster trains operated as expresses between New York and White Plains and made local stops between White Plains and Brewster. Trains to and from points north of Brewster stopped only at White Plains. Not all trains beyond Brewster went as far as Chatham; a few commuter trains tied up for the night at Pawling or Dover Plains or deadheaded to and from Brewster.

Steam operation on the Harlem Division ended September 11, 1952, when Pacific 4549 (Schenectady, 1912) brought train 18, Dover Plains to White Plains North. Less than two months before, on July 16, 1952, No. 4549 headed the last steam run on the West Shore.

Recommended reading:

The Coming of the New York and Harlem Railroad, by Louis V. Grogan, published in 1989 by Louis V. Grogan, 31 Sans Souci Drive, Pawling, NY 12564. ISBN 0-962120-65-0.

A 13-car train of old clerestory-roof multiple-unit cars rolls into the station at Bronxville to pick up Manhattan-bound commuters. New York Central photo.

A Grand Central-bound suburban train accelerates out of Hawthorne behind Alco RS-3
No. 8337. The diesel will haul the train to White Plains, where an electric locomotive will take
over for the rest of the run. Photo by William D. Middleton, June 1953.

Train 519 — Ten-Wheeler, combine, and coach — stands at Golden's Bridge waiting for Harlem Division train 19 to arrive from New York with connecting passengers and baggage for Lake Mahopac. Photo by John P. Ahrens.

Pacific 4531, a K-11, accelerates out of Brewster with train 18, a late-morning train from Pawling to Grand Central. Beyond the train is the East Branch of the Croton River. Photo by John P. Ahrens, March 19, 1949.

The ironwork of an ancient truss bridge between Golden's Bridge and Lincolndale frames Ten-Wheeler 1253. The bridge is doubtless one reason the 4-6-0 is the largest locomotive permitted on the line. Photo by John F. McBride.

New York Central's K-10 and K-11 Pacifics were 69-inch-drivered engines intended for freight service. A few of them, among them Boston & Albany 580, were given 72-inch drivers and reclassified K-14, but the higher drivers don't hinder 580's pulling power as it departs Brewster for Chatham. Dieselization of the B&A accounts for the presence of the subsidiary's locomotives on the parent's rails. Photo by John P. Ahrens, June 4, 1949.

Train 15, a New York-North Adams train, speeds under the New Haven's Maybrook line at Towners, with No. 4399 in charge. The Pacific is a K-14, but the Elesco feedwater heater mounted ahead of the smokebox and the cast trailing truck make it look more modern than B&A 580. Photo by John P. Ahrens, July 24, 1948.

Ten-Wheeler 820 leads an afternoon train from High Bridge into the station at Ardsley.
Photo by Theo. A. Gay, June 15, 1946.

PUTNAM DIVISION

Lying between the Hudson Division and the Harlem Division was the Putnam Division, which extended from 155th Street in The Bronx to Putnam Junction at Brewster. The Putnam Division had its roots in a railroad proposed to give Boston an alternate route to the West via the Erie Railway — known at various times as the Midland, the Boston, Hartford & Erie, and the New York & New England Railroad.

An obvious adjunct to this proposal was a branch to New York City. It would create an all-rail route between Boston and New York. Most Boston-New York traffic used a rail-water route — train from Boston to Providence, Fall River, or Newport, and boat beyond. The route that would become New Haven's Shore Line did not become a serious competitor in the Boston-New York market until 1889, when the Thames River was bridged at New London.

A group of New Yorkers incorporated the New York & Boston Railroad on May 21, 1869, to build a line from High Bridge, on the Harlem River in The Bronx, north through Westchester County to Brewster, just barely over the county line in Putnam County and about 4 miles west of the Connecticut state line. In addition to handling through business, the new line would help develop Westchester County. Farms along the way and an iron mine near Brewster would provide freight traffic. Even before construction in February 1870 there were proposals to extend the line south to Port Morris on the East River and to operate boats from High Bridge to the business center of New York City.

The New York & Boston then got caught up in a proposal for a New York-Montreal railroad made up of several small railroad companies, some already built and some not, between New York and Chatham, and the Rutland north of Chatham. It would be a line with an abundance of grades and curves paralleling for its entire length the route already long established by the New York Central and the Delaware & Hudson (to use latter-day names). The project would also give the Erie a foothold in New England, and to that end the Erie proposed a tunnel under the Hudson and a connection with the New York & Boston.

The Erie found the necessary funds for the tunnel; six railroads, including the New York & Northern, were consolidated as the New York, Boston & Montreal; and the Panic of 1873 hit. The proposal fell apart. The bondholders of the New York & Boston reorganized as the New York, Westchester & Putnam Railroad, then formed the New York City & Northern Railroad, to lease the roadbed of the New York & Northern and build tracks on it.

Two short additions were made as construction got under way — a 1-mile extension south from High Bridge to the north end of the elevated line at Eighth Avenue and 155th Street, and a 3-mile branch to Getty Square in Yonkers.

The High Bridge-Brewster line was opened from High Bridge to Brewster in December 1880. Initial schedules called for 5 hours for the 57-mile trip. Service soon speeded up, and in 1882 through service from High Bridge to Hartford, Connecticut, was established — two trains a day each way.

A line relocation in 1881 eliminated a fearsome trestle at East View, and in 1884 the Mahopac Iron Ore Company built a 4-mile line from Baldwin Place on the NYC&N through Mahopac Falls to Mahopac Mines. The branch was operated from the beginning by the NYC&N.

Financial difficulties overtook the railroad in 1882 and it entered receivership. It was sold at foreclosure in 1887 and became the New York & Northern Railway. The future of the new company depended on becoming part of a New York-Boston route in conjunction with the New York & New England, which was pretty much hemmed in by the New York, New Haven & Hartford. The Philadelphia & Reading, suddenly expanding into New England, took control of the NY&NE in 1893 and collapsed a few months later. The New Haven, which had its own route into New York, got the NY&NE. Milk traffic on the NY&N dwindled as a result of the creation of Croton Reservoir, which flooded much of the farmland, and the iron mines shut down. The only course remaining to the NY&N was for it to be enfolded by a large, strong railroad — the New York Central & Hudson River. The New York & Putnam Railroad was organized in 1894 to acquire the property of the New York & Northern and was then leased by the NYC&HR. The New York & Putnam was merged by the NYC&HR in 1913, and in 1914 the NYC&HR became the New York Central. The railroad settled down to a simple existence as a commuter carrier, even though Putnam trains never ran to and from Grand Central. Passengers could transfer to Hudson Division local trains at High Bridge and to elevated trains at Sedgwick Avenue.

In 1930 a major line relocation was undertaken between East View and Briarcliff Manor, shortening the line by 3 miles and eliminating a loop around Tarrytown Reservoir. The reason for the construction was that John D. Rockefeller, Jr., wanted to expand his estate and the Putnam Division ran through the property he wanted. The relocation eliminated three stations and considerable freight business and put the Putnam Division within a half mile of the Harlem Division. (As far north as Briarcliff Manor the Putnam was only two or three miles east of the Hudson Division.)

In the late 1920s NYC replaced a number of the steam-powered trains with gas-electric cars; the traffic surge of World War II required a return to steam and longer trains. Ten-Wheelers replaced 4-4-0s at the head of passenger trains — and NYC's F-12 class 4-6-0s were the heaviest locomotives allowed on the Putnam Division.

The Yonkers branch was electrified in 1926. Not long after electric service began, traffic on the branch went into a decline. A lift that connected one station with a residential area was taken out of service, and the elevated lines that the MU cars connected with in The Bronx were abandoned. Yonkers Branch service ended June 30, 1943.

Traffic continued to decline after World War II. NYC undertook some minor modernization in the form of electric lighting for the stations and diesel power for the trains — a group of Lima 1200-horsepower road switchers. The last steam-powered train ran on September 29, 1951. Ridership continue to decline, and while receipts went down, property taxes went up. In 1956 the New York Central proposed abandoning the branch.

The riders, quite naturally, protested, saying that express trains and through service to Grand Central Terminal would increase business. The Central's response was that express trains would antagonize passengers at stations where trains didn't stop, and through service was impossible because diesels couldn't go into Grand Central. Besides, it would cost too much to develop a diesel locomotive that could also operate as a straight electric from the third rail. More than that, a second crew would have been required for the 7 miles from High Bridge to Grand Central, because the unions objected to interdivisional crew assignments.

It's worth noting that NYC bought 35 dual-power locomotives in 1930 and used them in electrified-zone switching service until the late 1940s, and in 1956 the New Haven received its first FL9s, diesels that could run straight into Grand Central drawing power from the third rail. The alternative of changing engines at High Bridge for the run into Grand Central evidently wasn't considered. Such a short run wasn't without precedent — consider all those empty passenger trains that shuttled between between Grand Central and the coach yards at Mott Haven. The problem of interdivisional runs disappeared soon after passenger service ended when the Putnam Division ceased to be a separate division.

The Public Service Commission allowed NYC to cut service on the Putnam Division in half and raise fares 15 percent. NYC asked Westchester County to contribute to the operating costs; the county said it couldn't use public money to help the New York Central. The last run was on May 29, 1958.

Recommended reading:

The Putnam Division, by Daniel R. Gallo and Frederick A. Kramer, published in 1981 by Quadrant Press, 19 West 44th Street, New York, NY 10036. ISBN 0-915276-29-1.

A brand-new Lima-Hamilton 1200-horsepower road switcher has replaced the expected
Ten-Wheeler at Briarcliff Manor on a northbound Sunday morning train.
Photo by Bert Pennypacker, July 15, 1951.

Engine 1270, also a Ten-Wheeler, stands at Briarcliff Manor's Tudor-styled station while passengers detrain. Shirtsleeves and open windows give evidence that it's a warm afternoon. Photo by Fielding L. Bowman, 1948.

Ten-Wheeler 1237, built by Schenectady in 1906, departs Brewster for Lake Mahopac with train 518, a Sunday-afternoon train to Grand Central via Golden's Bridge and the Harlem Division.

Ferries plied the Hudson River between West Shore's terminal at Weehawken and two terminals in Manhattan — at West 42nd Street, directly across from Weehawken, and at Cortlandt Street, about 4 miles downriver. New York Central photo.

West Shore

In 1880 the Vanderbilt empire was suddenly plagued by nuisance railroads, railroads built alongside its lines to siphon away traffic. The New York, Chicago & St. Louis Railway, which grew out of a disagreement between the Lake Erie & Western and the Lake Shore & Michigan Southern, was incorporated to build a line between Cleveland and Buffalo, right alongside the LS&MS. The New York, West Shore & Buffalo was proposed, surveyed, and organized to parallel the New York Central & Hudson River from New York to Buffalo — up the west bank of the Hudson, then along the south bank of the Mohawk. For much of the distance from New York to Utica the West Shore was within sight of the NYC&HR.

The area west of the Hudson was generally without railroads. A few lines had been built west into the mountains, but people living along the west bank who wanted to go north to Albany or south to New York had to take a boat — at the very least, across the river to the NYC&HR. The organizers of the West Shore felt there was enough New York-Albany-Buffalo traffic to support a second railroad; the NYC&HR felt the same way but didn't intend to give up any of that traffic.

The south end of the West Shore was put together by combining the Jersey City & Albany Railroad, which had a 38-mile line from Weehawken, New Jersey, to Fort Montgomery, New York, and the North River Railway, which was chartered to build a line from Fort Montgomery to Albany, with a branch to Middletown. Because the Jersey City & Albany was controlled by the New York, Ontario & Western Railway, the line between Weehawken and Cornwall was constructed and operated jointly, and NYO&W later had trackage rights over that line.

The West Shore purchased the Athens Branch of the NYC&HR (formerly the Saratoga & Hudson River Railway, acquired by the NYC&HR in 1867), a line from Schenectady southeast to Athens, on the Hudson River opposite the city of Hudson.

Track and right of way

The West Shore was well engineered. Much of the route was alongside the Hudson and therefore level. The part that wasn't had negligible grades. In later years the line was four tracks wide from Weehawken to Dumont, 13 miles, and double track from there to Ravena, just south of Albany.

Because there was no room between the base of the Palisades and the river, the West Shore left Weehawken through a tunnel, then turned north through North Bergen, Ridgefield, Norwood, and West Nyack before moving back to the riverbank through another tunnel south of Haverstraw. Several tunnels were necessary along the river farther north; one was built directly under the parade ground at the United States Military Academy at West Point. The line turned inland again at West Park, across the river from Hyde Park, then paralleled the river at a distance of about 2 miles from there north to Ravena.

Branches and connections

The West Shore connected with other railroads along the New Jersey waterfront through the New Jersey Junction Railroad, which had a 4.4-mile line extending south from Weehawken to connect with the Lackawanna, the Erie, and the Pennsylvania. The road was leased by the NYC in 1886. As far north as Orangeburg, New York, the West Shore lay between two subsidiaries of the Erie — the Northern Railroad of New Jersey on the east and the New Jersey & New York on the west. At Orangeburg it crossed the Erie's original line west from the Hudson at Piermont, and at West Haverstraw it met the north end of the New Jersey & New York. The next junction was at Cornwall, where New York, Ontario & Western trains diverged onto their own line. At Newburgh the West Shore met a pair of Erie branches from Greycourt and Harriman (they joined a few miles west of Newburgh).

At Highland, opposite Poughkeepsie, the West Shore was only 200 feet or so from the New Haven's Maybrook Line, but the separation was vertical and there was no track connection. Kingston, the largest city on the west bank of the Hudson between Newburgh and Albany, was a busy junction. There the West Shore met a branch of the New York, Ontario & Western from Port Jervis and Summitville, NYC's branch from Campbell Hall (the former Wallkill Valley Railroad, absorbed by the NYC&HR in 1899), and the Ulster & Delaware to Oneonta (which became part of the NYC in 1932). At Ravena the main line turned west toward Buffalo; Albany was on a single-track branch, and the last 1.4 miles to Albany Union Station were on Delaware & Hudson rails.

Traffic and operation

The West Shore was not the passenger carrier that the Hudson Division was. It was an obvious choice for passengers traveling between northern New Jersey and towns along the west bank of the Hudson, but passengers from New York to west-bank destinations could often do better by riding the Hudson Division north, then crossing the river by ferry. For New York-Albany trips, the West Shore was significantly slower and much less frequent.

In 1930 there were eight trains each way between Weehawken and Albany — five locals (they ran as expresses south of West Point) and three semifast trains. A few trains carried parlor-buffet cars. By 1948 through service was down to four locals and one fast train, the latter primarily a carrier of mail and express.

The south end of the West Shore was suburban territory. Commuter trains from Weehawken terminated at Dumont, West Haverstraw, and Newburgh. The peak year for commuter traffic was 1927. The opening of the George Washington Bridge in 1931 gave New Jerseyites two more ways to get to work — car and bus — and cut severely into the West Shore's traffic. Ridership continued to decline, and by 1958 the commuter trains carried only about 5900 passengers each day. NYC was losing money on the service. On March 24, 1959, NYC discontinued the ferries that carried commuters from Weehawken to Cortlandt Street and West 42nd Street in Manhattan. That made the West Shore's commuter trains suitable only for people who worked in Weehawken, and ridership dropped to 200 passengers a day. NYC discontinued the trains on December 10, 1959. The state of New Jersey ordered NYC to operate five trains a day to the Lackawanna terminal in Hoboken, but to no avail, since the Interstate Commerce Commission had given NYC permission to drop the trains.

The West Shore's lack of passenger traffic and its waterfront terminal made it an ideal freight route into metropolitan New York, especially northern New Jersey. Its line west from Ravena to the Mohawk Valley bypassed Albany and Schenectady and became the nucleus of the Castleton Cutoff.

The highway bridges and tunnels that drew passenger business away from the West Shore increased its importance as a freight carrier. The tight clearances along the Hudson Division and the cramped location of the West Side Freight Line were not well suited to traffic moving in containers and trailers, but the West Shore had ample clearances and there was plenty of room in northern New Jersey for transfer facilities.

Recommended reading:

Rails Along the Hudson, edited by Thomas M. Crawford and Frederick A. Kramer, published in 1979 by Quadrant Press, 19 West 44th Street, New York, NY 10036. ISBN 0-915276-25-9.

West Shore's Weehawken terminal was located on a narrow strip of level land between the base of the Palisades and the Hudson River. Above is the large freight yard where trains were made up and broken apart for transfer to the other railroads along the New Jersey waterfront. At right is the passenger station and ferry terminal — architecturally no match for Grand Central. Above, photo by David Plowden, March 1957; right, Ewing Galloway photo.

Pacific 4539, a K-11, whose footboards in place of a genuine pilot indicate its primarily role as a local freight and switching engine, gets under way from Claremont (2 miles south of Jersey City) with a transfer freight from the Central Railroad of New Jersey. Photo by Robert P. Morris, October 30, 1948.

Mikado 3787 has a fast freight rolling northward at Little Ferry, New Jersey. The 2-8-2 is an H-5, rebuilt by Alco's Brooks Works from a 2-8-0 in 1913. Photo by M. B. Cooke.

The short consist following Mohawk 3020 at West Englewood includes two French 2-8-2s
built by Alco at Schenectady. Photo by Harold H. Carstens.

A northbound passenger train enters the double-track Haverstraw tunnel, which will take it to the west bank of the Hudson. Photo by J. W. Woodruff, May 31, 1947.

An Alco RS-3 is the power for a southbound passenger train as it passes under the west end of the Bear Mountain Bridge south of Fort Montgomery. Photo by Elmer Treloar, June 4, 1953.

Two former Ulster & Delaware 4-6-0s join forces to move symbol freight RV-9 on the Walkill Valley branch at Montgomery. When NYC bought the U&D in 1932 it acquired 22 Ten-Wheelers of antiquated design (only two years previously NYC was buying 4-6-4s, 2-8-4s, and 4-8-2s). Most of them remained active until 1949. Photo by Donald W. Furler.

The square sand dome of Hudson 5456 is an immediate clue that this isn't one of NYC's own but rather former Boston & Albany 601, given a reprieve on the West Shore after the dieselization of the B&A. The train is passing the Selkirk station, heading for Weehawken. Baxter & Allen photo.

At the south end of the elevated line was the new St. John's Park freight terminal. A tri-power locomotive is emerging from the building. The track in the street at the left is for city streetcars, which drew power from a third rail located in a conduit in the center of the track. NYC photo, 1934.

WEST SIDE FREIGHT LINE

Vanderbilt's intention in building Grand Central Depot was to have a single monumental station for the trains of both his railroads, the New York & Harlem and the Hudson River. The importance of the Hudson River Railroad line down the west side of Manhattan declined as far as passenger business was concerned. (Local trains lasted until World War I but by 1900 were no longer mentioned in the *Official Guide*.) At the same time its importance increased for freight service. The route into Grand Central was useless for freight, because it was in a tunnel most of the way. The West Side Line was at ground level and lay within a block or two of the Hudson River piers — indeed it was the only other railroad on Manhattan Island. (The Pennsylvania Railroad line across Manhattan, opened in 1910, had no rail connection to street level in Manhattan — indeed, was open to the sky for only a block or two of its length.) The West Side Line became the primary route into New York City for mail, express, and perishable foodstuffs, particularly dairy products and live poultry.

Trains coming down the Hudson Division heading for the West Side Line kept going straight ahead at Spuyten Duyvil, where the passenger line turned sharply to the east. They crossed Spuyten Duyvil Creek on a drawbridge, then stayed close to the east bank of the river as far south as 60th Street Yard, the major classification facility and engine terminal on the line. The entire line was double track.

Between 60th Street and 30th Street the tracks were originally located in Eleventh Avenue; they were in Tenth Avenue and Marginal Way south of 30th Street. By law trains operating in the streets were restricted to 6 mph and had to be preceded by a flagman riding a horse. In the mid-1920s the New York Central undertook a line relocation project. The first phase, opened in 1934, was to elevate the line south of 30th Street Yard. The project included a new freight terminal at Spring Street, abandonment of the line in Canal and Hudson Streets south of there, depression of the tracks between 60th Street and 30th Street, a new yard below street level at 33rd Street, electrification of the line from Spuyten Duyvil to 23rd Street, and elimination of steam locomotives for switching by the use of tri-power locomotives (diesel-electric/straight electric/battery).

In early years for service in the streets NYC used "dummy" locomotives, four-wheel and six-wheel steam switchers shrouded to look like a passenger car. Apparently horses were frightened by conventional steam locomotives, but a passenger car emitting smoke, steam, and noise didn't bother them. In 1923 NYC bought five two-truck Shays, also shrouded, to replace the 0-4-0s and 0-6-0s.

The West Side Line was electrified and dieselized to eliminate the smoke nuisance of steam locomotives. After diesel power replaced steam on mainline freight trains it made little sense to change to electric locomotives at Harmon, and New York Central turned off the power to the third rail in 1959.

This view looks south along the elevated line from the Cudahy and Armour plants at 14th Street. The large building over the track in the middle distance is the Manhattan Refrigerating Company; beyond it is the Bell Telephone Laboratories building. In the distance are the skyscrapers of lower Manhattan. NYC photo, 1934.

The elevated line was brand new in this photo taken looking north. The street visible closest to the camera is West 18th Street. NYC photo.

Trains operating in the streets were required to be preceded by a flagman on horseback. The cowboy is riding the range at Tenth Avenue and West 18th Street. The large building in the background houses the Merchants Refrigerating Company. Engine 529 is one of 35 tri-power locomotives (diesel-electric/straight electric/battery) that General Electric built for New York Central in 1930. In third-rail territory they operated as straight electrics and charged their batteries; away from third rail they drew traction power from the batteries, and the diesel engines charged the batteries. NYC photo, 1941.

An unlikely sight at the corner of 11th Avenue and West 30th Street is RS3 No. 8350 with the Empire State Building beyond. Photo by Jim Shaughnessy, April 13, 1957.

The tracks branching to the right just beyond the smokestack continue south; those beyond also turn right and enter the post office. Photo by Jim Shaughnessy, April 13, 1957.

This high-level view of 30th Street Yard clearly shows the elevated main line heading south and the tracks entering the post office at the left. The Pennsylvania Railroad's Hudson River tunnels run underneath the yard from lower left to middle right. NYC photo, about 1934.

The 30th Street yard had team tracks where fruit and vegetables could be unloaded directly from refrigerator cars to trucks. Photo by Jim Shaughnessy, April 13, 1957.

From 60th Street south to 30th Street the West Side Line was below street level. This fireman's-eye view shows that for much of that distance the line lay in a rock cut. Photo by Jim Shaughnessy, April 13, 1957.

Automatic block signaling was used only on the northernmost 4 miles of the West Side Line. Below St. Clair Place (in the West 120s) switches were thrown by hand and train movements were controlled by hand signals. Photo by Jim Shaughnessy, April 13, 1957.

A southbound train approaches the George Washington Bridge. The roadbed gives evidence that the line was once four tracks wide here. Photo by Jim Shaughnessy, April 13, 1957.

The swing bridge over Spuyten Duyvil Creek at the north end of the West Side Line was operated by steam. Photo by David Plowden, November 1961.

The rails of the West Shore are kept shiny by Conrail freights. Amtrak uses the West Side Freight Line to reach Penn Station, and its trains speed along the upper end of the Hudson Division faster than NYC did. Metro-North continues the task of carrying commuters. In 1983 and 1984 Metro-North rebuilt and electrified the Harlem Division line between White Plains and Brewster. Most of Metro-North's trains are made up of MU cars like these, shown on a curve south of Croton Falls. Photo by Scott Hartley, May 5, 1984.

THE LINES TODAY

Even though the bulk of its traffic was commuters, Grand Central Terminal seemed to mirror the decline of long-distance passenger train travel and then the decline of its owner after 1968, Penn Central. When Amtrak began operation in 1971, the most distant destination Grand Central could offer was Buffalo, but later Amtrak added trains to Chicago, Detroit, and Montreal. On April 7, 1991, Amtrak moved its trains from Grand Central to Penn Station, making Grand Central exclusively a commuter station.

The building itself was threatened by proposals to erect office buildings on air rights. The Pan Am building was built just north of Grand Central in 1964, its 59-story glass façade contrasting with the Beaux Arts style of Grand Central. Worse, there was a proposal to erect a building right over the waiting room and concourse. Grand Central was designated a city landmark in 1967, and in 1978 that designation was upheld by the U. S. Supreme Court. In recent years Grand Central's lessee and operator, Metro-North Railroad, has undertaken and completed a restoration of the building and the Park Avenue Tunnel.

The Hudson Division is alive and well. Much of the track has been rebuilt in recent years, permitting higher speeds for Amtrak trains. Metro-North runs electric commuter trains between Grand Central and Croton-Harmon and diesel-powered trains between Croton-Harmon and Poughkeepsie (the Croton-on-Hudson and Harmon stations were combined). Amtrak operates frequent service between New York and Albany; trains continue to Montreal, Buffalo, Toronto, and Chicago.

Albany Union Station was closed in 1968 to make way for a highway; the building remains in use as a bank. Penn Central shifted its passenger operations to a new station east of the river in Rensselaer. All traffic was shifted to the northerly of the two bridges over the Hudson. Amtrak later built a new station in Rensselaer.

Harlem Division passenger service north of Dover Plains ended abruptly on March 20, 1972. The service consisted of a single train down from Chatham in the morning and back in the late afternoon. The morning train ran from Chatham to New York as usual. During the day Penn Central received permission to drop the train. The return trip that evening ran only to Dover Plains; passengers and crew living north of there had to make their own arrangements to get home. The last freight train on the line between Chatham and Dover Plains ran on March 27, 1976.

Commuter service south of Dover Plains was operated first by Penn Central, then Conrail, with subsidy from the Metropolitan Transportation Authority. Metro-North Commuter Railroad, a subsidiary of MTA, took over the operation from Conrail on January 1, 1983. By then work had already begun on extending the electrification north from White Plains to Brewster, accompanied by new high-level platforms at each station. Electric service to Brewster North, a station easily reached from Interstate 84, began on June 8, 1984. Diesel-hauled trains shuttle between Brewster North and Dover Plains several times a day. The track remains in place for freight service between Dover Plains and Wassaic, about 5 miles.

The Putnam Division was useful for high and wide loads into New York until clearances were improved on the West Shore line. In 1962 the 23 miles between East View and Lake Mahopac were abandoned. The portion from Lake Mahopac to Brewster was abandoned in 1969 and 1970. The south end of the line remained in service some years longer.

The West Shore is Conrail's principal freight line into the New York area from the north. It has become largely single track.

Conrail ceased using the West Side Freight Line in 1983. In order to consolidate its New York operations at a single station and facilitate connections between the New York State services and the Northeast Corridor, Amtrak refurbished the track of the West Side Line and constructed a connection from the West Side Line at 37th Street to the south side of Pennsylvania Station. The connection passes under the Long Island Rail Road's storage tracks west of Penn Station and over Amtrak's Hudson River tunnels. It is electrified from 38th Street to Penn Station with the over-running third rail system used in Penn Station.

INDEX OF PHOTOGRAPHS

Locations
Albany: 80-83
Ardsley: 96
Bear Mountain Bridge: 56-58, 110
Breakneck Mountain: 64-66
Brewster: 92, 94, 101
Briarcliff Manor: 100, 101
Bronxville: 90
Camelot: cover, 4, 68, 69
Claremont, N. J.: 108
Croton Falls: 124
Garrison to Cold Spring: 59-61, 63
Golden's Bridge: 92, 93
Grand Central Terminal: 10, 14-17
Haverstraw: 110
Hawthorne: 91
Hudson River: 102
Little Ferry, N. J.: 108
Manhattan (West Side) 112, 115-122
Montgomery: 111
Mott Haven to Spuyten Duyvil: 23, 26, 30-35, 123
Oscawanna and Crugers: 47-52
Park Avenue Tunnel and Viaduct: 18-22
Peekskill: 53-55
Poughkeepsie: 69
Rhinecliff to Castleton: 70-75, 77
Selkirk: 76, 101
Spuyten Duyvil to Harmon: 36-44, 46, 62
Storm King Mountain: 67
Towners: 95
Troy: 78, 79
Weehawken: 106, 107
West Englewood, N. J.: 109
White Plains: 84

Diesel locomotives
E7 No. 4002: 68
E7 No. 4003: 68
E7 No. 4006: 61
E7 No. 4007: 62
E7 No. 4013: 63
E7 No. 4022: 70
E7 No. 4023: 41
E7 No. 4025: 70
E7 No. 4034: 62
E7 No. 4016: 83
E8 No. 4060: 69
E8 No. 4062: 82
E8 No. 4089: 80
Erie-built No. 4400: 66
Erie-built No. 4403: 43
F7 No. 1810: 51
FA-2 No. 1091: 50
Lima-Hamilton 1200-hp No. 5814: 100
PA-1 No. 4202: 62
PA-1 No. 4209: 59
RS-3 No. 8216: 41
RS-3 No. 8337: 91
RS-3 No. 8350: 117, 118
S-4 No. 8591
Tri-power No. 529: 116
RDCs: 41, 42

Electric locomotives and cars
No. 117: 23
No. 131: 22
No. 222: 24, 26, 31
No. 223: 18
No. 224: 23
No. 226: 35, 36
No. 232: 42
No. 235: 17
No. 254: 30
No. 275: 35
No. 278: 38

No. 282: 39
No. 1174: 25
No. 3424: 24
MU cars: 19, 21, 30, 32, 33, 34, 40, 84, 90, 124

Steam locomotives
2-8-2 No. 3787: 108
4-6-0 No. 806: 111
4-6-0 No. 820: 96
4-6-0 No. 857: 92
4-6-0 No. 1237: 101
4-6-0 No. 1253: 93
4-6-0 No. 1270: 101
4-6-2 No. 580 (B&A): 94
4-6-2 No. 4399: 95
4-6-2 No. 4531: 92
4-6-2 No. 4537: 36
4-6-2 No. 4539: 108
4-6-2 No. 4569: 67
4-6-2 No. 4742: 44
4-6-4 No. 5202: 49
4-6-4 No. 5204: 56
4-6-4 No. 5210: 76
4-6-4 No. 5222: 68
4-6-4 No. 5226: 53
4-6-4 No. 5255: 52
4-6-4 No. 5265: cover, 4
4-6-4 No. 5269: 53
4-6-4 No. 5297: 45
4-6-4 No. 5298: 70
4-6-4 No. 5303: 54
4-6-4 No. 5311: 54
4-6-4 No. 5328: 71
4-6-4 No. 5420: 47
4-6-4 No. 5423: 46
4-6-4 No. 5426: 64
4-6-4 No. 5451: 47
4-6-4 No. 5453: 53
4-6-4 No. 5456: 111
4-8-2 No. 2742: 77
4-8-2 No. 2890: 65

4-8-2 No. 3020: 109
4-8-2 No. 3115: 72
4-8-2 No. 3148: 48
4-8-4 No. 6012: 69
4-8-4 No. 6017: 43, 55
4-8-4 No. 6019: 49
4-8-4 No. 6020: 73

Photographers
Ahrens, John P.: cover, 4, 68, 69, 92, 94, 95, 101
Baxter, Gene: 78, 111
Bennett, James D.: 55
Bovid, C. M.: 66
Bowman, Fielding L.: 101
Brumbaugh, Wayne: 54, 56, 60
Carstens, Harold H.: 109
Cooke, M. B.: 108
Curtis, W. W.: 47
Dawson, E. B., Jr.: 21
Donahue, T. J.: 65
Eidenbenz, F.: 58
Furler, Donald W.: 111
Galloway, Ewing: 107
Gay, Theo A.: 47-49, 96
Hartley, Scott: 124
Harwood, Herbert H., Jr.: 18, 23, 26, 30-32, 35
Hastings, Philip R.: 81
Henry, Raymond C.: 67, 70
Knauer, Arthur F.: 36
Link, O. Winston: 57
Malinoski, Robert R.: 61
McBride, John F.: 52, 59, 93
Middleton, William D., 71, 76, 91
Morris, Robert P.: 108
New York Central: 10, 14, 15, 19, 63, 64, 74, 77, 84, 90, 102, 112, 115, 116, 119
Pennypacker, Bert: 50, 100

Pickett, John: 34, 36, 37
Plowden, David: 16, 21, 22, 38, 39, 41, 106, 123
Quin, Frank: 43, 46, 49
Quinn, Joseph R.: 70
Rinke, Herman: 33
Salter, David W.: 51
Shaughnessy, Jim: 17, 20, 30, 34, 40, 42, 43, 69, 75, 79, 80, 82, 83, 117, 118, 120-122
Tobey, R. E.: 72, 73
Treloar, Elmer: 110
Weisberger, Herb: 53
Woodruff, J. W.: 110

Passenger trains
Advance Commodore Vanderbilt: 49
Advance Knickerbocker: 49
Cleveland Limited: 22
Commodore Vanderbilt: 57
Empire State Express: 17, 36, 64, 83
Fifth Avenue: 22
Knickerbocker: 23, 38, 66, 69
Lake Shore Limited: cover, 4, 26
Laurentian: 42, 56, 73, 79, 81
Missourian: 39, 68
Mohawk: 70, 71
Niagara: 54
North Shore Limited: 43, 70, 75
Ohio State Limited: 47
Pacemaker: 18, 31, 34, 35, 46, 80, 82
20th Century Limited: 22, 37, 47, 59-61, 63
Upstate Special: 55